THE KIDS' SIMPLE GUIDE TO PDA

by the same authors

The Educator's Experience of Pathological Demand Avoidance
An Illustrated Guide to Pathological Demand Avoidance and Learning
Laura Kerbey
Illustrated by Eliza Fricker
ISBN 978 1 83997 696 4
eISBN 978 1 83997 698 8

The Teen's Guide to Pathological Demand Avoidance
Laura Kerbey
Foreword by Dr Julia Woollatt
Illustrated by Eliza Fricker
ISBN 978 1 80501 183 5
eISBN 978 1 80501 184 2

The Family Experience of PDA
An Illustrated Guide to Pathological Demand Avoidance
Eliza Fricker
ISBN 978 1 78775 677 9
eISBN 978 1 78775 678 6

Can't Not Won't
A Story About a Child Who Couldn't Go to School
Eliza Fricker
ISBN 978 1 83997 520 2
eISBN 978 1 83997 521 9

Thumbsucker
An Illustrated Journey Through an Undiagnosed Autistic Childhood
Eliza Fricker
ISBN 978 1 83997 854 8
eISBN 978 1 83997 855 5

The KIDS' SIMPLE GUIDE to PDA

LAURA KERBEY
AND ELIZA FRICKER
Illustrated by ELIZA FRICKER

Jessica Kingsley Publishers
London and Philadelphia

First published in Great Britain in 2025 by Jessica Kingsley Publishers
An imprint of John Murray Press

Front cover image source: Eliza Fricker. The cover image is for illustrative purposes only, and any person featuring is a model.

A CIP catalogue record for this title is available from the British Library and the Library of Congress

ISBN 978 1 80501 815 5
eISBN 978 1 80501 816 2

Printed and bound in Great Britain by Clays Ltd

Jessica Kingsley Publishers' policy is to use papers that are natural, renewable and recyclable products and made from wood grown in sustainable forests. The logging and manufacturing processes are expected to conform to the environmental regulations of the country of origin.

Jessica Kingsley Publishers
Carmelite House
50 Victoria Embankment
London EC4Y 0DZ

www.jkp.com

John Murray Press
Part of Hodder & Stoughton Ltd
An Hachette Company

The authorised representative in the EEA is Hachette Ireland,
8 Castlecourt Centre, Dublin 15, D15 XTP3, Ireland (email: info@hbgi.ie)

This book is dedicated to all the amazing young people with PDA and their equally amazing siblings that I have had the pleasure of working with over the years.

Also, to Rocket, my favourite writing companion.

Acknowledgements

Thank you to all the amazing children and young people with PDA and the families that I have had the pleasure of working with over the years. You constantly inspire me to write books like this to help others understand the complexities and highs and lows of PDA.

Thank you as always to my friend and illustrator Eliza for making the process of book writing as fun, collaborative and low-demand as possible.

Thank you to everyone at JKP for your continued support.

CONTENTS

A Note to Parents

We hope that this book will be a helpful, positive and informative guide for siblings, other family members and friends of PDAers. Although they can read it alone, it may be valuable to read it with your child so that you can explore their understanding and feelings about PDA together. Throughout the book the Question Mark icon will provide opportunities to discuss various aspects of living with PDAers together.

Chapter 1

What is PDA?

Strong Interests

HUMOUR

SENSORY

ANXIOUS

WHAT IS PDA ?

AUTISTIC

CHARISMATIC

COMMUNICATION

Welcome to this book, 'The Kids' Simple Guide to PDA'.

You have probably been given this book to read as you have a brother or sister who has PDA. Or perhaps you are reading this because you have a cousin or friend who has PDA.

Whatever your relationship is to someone with PDA, it is brilliant that you are reading this book so that you can understand PDA a little more.

Having a better understanding of PDA will hopefully mean you understand the person with PDA in your life much better too, and this in turn should make your relationship with them even better.

PDA stands for Pathological Demand Avoidance.

PDA is a type of autism, so if someone has PDA, it also means that they are autistic.

If someone is autistic, or PDA, it also means that they are neurodivergent.

Neurodivergent is a term we use for anyone whose brain works differently from a neurotypical brain. (Neurotypical is the way we describe the most common type of brain.) Other types of neurodiversity that you may have already heard of include:

- ADHD
- dyslexia
- dysgraphia
- Tourette's Syndrome.

Here are some famous neurodivergent people you may have heard of:

- Simone Biles, who is an amazing gymnast, has ADHD.
- Greta Thunberg, who is an environmental activist, is autistic.
- Will.i.am, who is a musician and producer, has ADHD.
- Ryan Gosling, who is an actor, has ADHD.
- Tom Holland, who is also an actor, is dyslexic.
- Hannah Gadbsy, who is a comedian, is autistic.

This list could go on and on!

Do you know of any other famous people who are neurodivergent?

Now, all human beings are unique and special in some way. Sometimes we can see the differences that humans have – for example, different skin, hair or eye colour. We can also see different heights, body types and some disabilities.

We cannot usually see when someone is neurodivergent, and this can be confusing as we may not always understand why a neurodivergent person finds some things extremely hard. You can look at someone with PDA and not know that they have PDA, even if it's very much a part of who they are.

But it is also important to remember that if someone is neurodivergent then there is **nothing** wrong with them. If a neurodivergent person is struggling, it is usually because there is something wrong with the environment that they are in and that is making them feel unsafe, uncomfortable or scared.

If someone is autistic, then it means that they experience, see and feel the world differently to non-autistic or neurotypical people.

Autistic people may find social situations extremely hard as it can be difficult for them to understand what people are **really** saying.

Autistic people may find it hard when things change unexpectedly.

We all have senses (such as how we see, hear and taste things around us), but autistic people might experience these differently. They may notice things around them that others don't. Sensory differences may include:

- finding some noises that others would not notice unbearably loud
- not being able to wear certain clothing because it feels scratchy or very uncomfortable
- finding some smells too strong, to the point that they make you feel sick
- not being able to eat certain foods due to taste or texture
- not being able to be in busy, loud places
- finding some lights too bright.

Everyone who is autistic has a different set of sensory difficulties and needs, but this can really affect how autistic people behave because they will avoid or seek things that help them feel safer and more comfortable.

People with PDA may have difficulties with all of the above as they are autistic.

As well as this, people with PDA find it really, really hard when they are asked, told or expected to do something. This is because it makes them feel really anxious when they don't have something called **autonomy**. This is the ability to make your own decisions. When they don't have autonomy, people with PDA feel that they are out of control, and we will talk a bit more about that in the next chapter.

The best way to explain autonomy is that it means 'self-driven'.

When you are older you may want to learn to drive a car. Now imagine if you were driving a car and the passenger next to you kept making unhelpful comments about your driving. Initially this may just be annoying, but if the passenger started grabbing the wheel and changing the direction of the car you would start to feel really anxious and then probably get quite angry! You would probably pull your car over and tell them to get out!

This is what it is like for someone with PDA. They need to be autonomous or self-driven most of the time; and if someone prevents this, they will become very anxious. The more anxious someone with PDA gets, then the more control they try to get back. (We are going to talk about anxiety later in this book.)

For someone with PDA, it is not just extreme situations like losing control of a car that make them feel anxious. Their anxiety can be triggered by things that other people would consider really tiny and easy to do, like choosing what to wear or eat, or having to follow a simple instruction. These things can cause just as much anxiety and are just as upsetting as things that appear as difficult as the 'big' triggers.

Mind the bus
That way
Mind that

I have water if you need it.

Other important things to understand about PDA include:

- Being very sensitive to facial expressions and tone of voice. This means that they can think that people are angry or shouting at them when they may not have been.

- Not always seeing the difference between themselves and adults. This means that they may not understand why a teacher or a parent can tell them to do things just because they are the grown-up.

- Preferring things to be novel and spontaneous, as when things become a routine they can feel like a demand.

The last thing to say about PDA in this chapter is that people with PDA are not choosing to avoid demands. Sometimes they really want to do things, but they just can't, and this must be incredibly frustrating for them, and you sometimes too.

A good way to think about PDA is to think:

It's 'I CAN'T (do it)' not 'I WON'T (do it)'.

Chapter 2

How Does Having PDA Make People Feel?

To understand how PDA makes people feel, we first need to understand what demands are and how demands make them feel.

Here are some examples of demands that people may make:

- 'Go and have a bath.'
- 'You need to do your homework.'
- 'It's time for you to go to bed now.'

Some demands are silent, they are expectations that aren't necessarily spoken out loud. For example:

- rules of games
- rules of how to behave
- social rules, such as manners

- routines such as dinner time, bed-time or leaving the house to go to school or an activity.

Some demands are ones that we create for ourselves:

- I need to do really well in this test.
- I need to go to sleep now.
- I should have a bath tonight.

Now, you probably don't like being told what to do (no one does really!). You may not like it when your mum or dad tells you to go to bed or do your homework. When you are told to do something, you may feel annoyed or angry, and you may sometimes argue back.

For someone with PDA, demands do not just make them feel annoyed or angry, they make them feel incredibly anxious because they feel that they have lost the autonomy that is so important to them. This makes them feel out of control and scared.

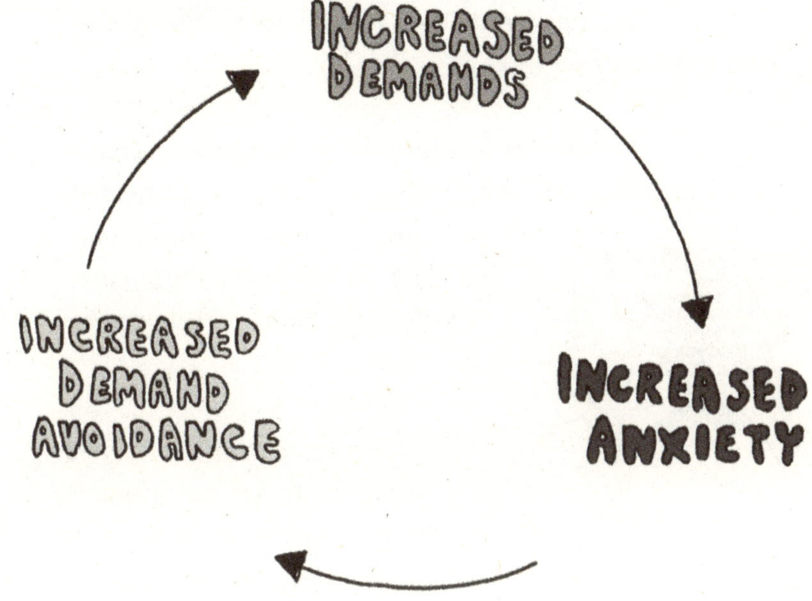

As we said in Chapter 1, try to remember that someone with PDA is not usually choosing to avoid demands. When somewhen tells a PDAer to do something it will make them feel so anxious that they won't be able to do the thing that they have been asked or told to do.

Remember, they are thinking:

'I CAN'T do this' not 'I WON'T do this'.

The other important thing to understand is that people with PDA feel anxious about demands they place on themselves too. This means that sometimes they cannot do the things they **want** to do as well as the things they **don't want** to do.

This is very frustrating for the person with PDA. It could mean that they get really excited about doing something, or going somewhere, but the demands build up and then their brain just tells them **No!** And they can't do it.

This means that sometimes you may also miss out on doing things or going places as the person you care about with PDA cannot manage to go anymore. It is OK for you to feel upset and disappointed about this too.

Can you remember a time that the person you cared about with PDA was not able to do something that they were looking forward to?

People with PDA have said that sometimes it feels like they have a battle going on inside of them when they want to do something very badly but just can't.

This means that people with PDA can sometimes feel very bad about themselves.

- They may feel angry with themselves.
- They may feel guilty that they have let people down.
- They may feel frustrated that they can't do things that they want to do.

- Or they may feel embarrassed that they can't do things that other people appear to be able to do easily.

If someone with PDA is feeling angry, guilty, frustrated or embarrassed it is important that we show them that we understand that they are feeling this way and don't say anything to make them feel worse.

Finally, when someone has PDA, it does not mean that they avoid **all** demands **all** the time. PDAers can do lots of things when their anxiety is low and when they see the point of what they have been asked or told to do. If they don't see the point, or they are too anxious, the demand will feel almost impossible to them.

High Anxiety = Lower Demand

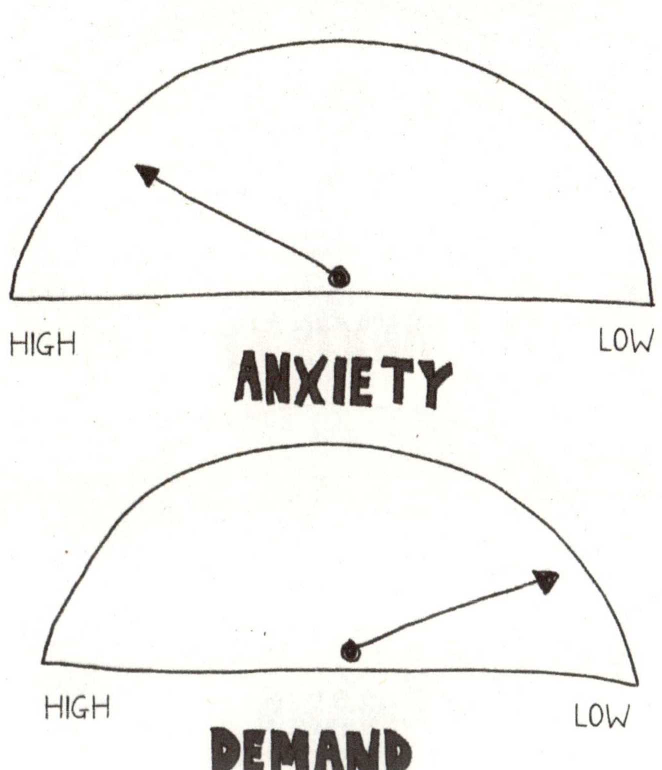

Lower Anxiety = Higher Demand

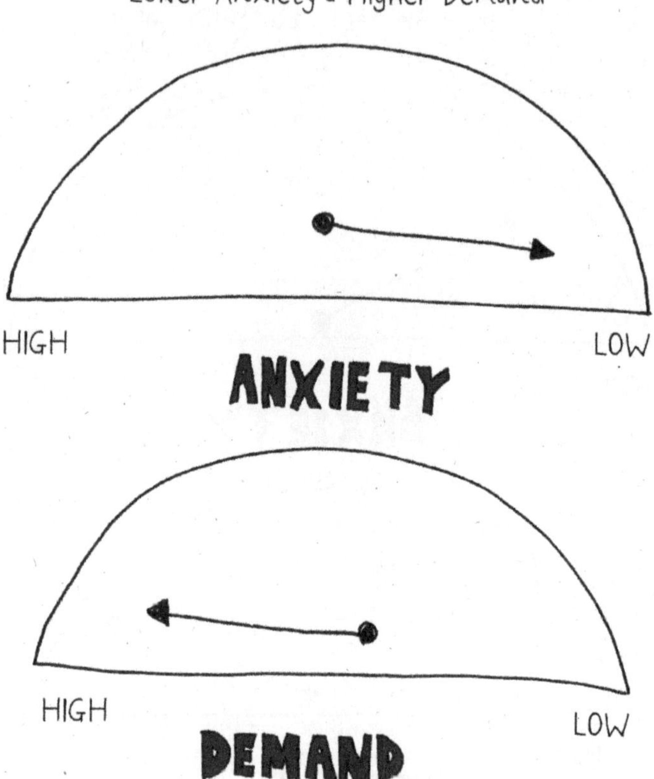

Chapter 3

PDA and Anxiety

To understand PDA, we have to understand the anxiety that people who have PDA are experiencing so much of the time.

Other words for feeling anxious include:

- worried
- nervous
- scared
- triggered.

Anxiety is not always a bad emotion all the time because our anxiety keeps us safe. It's a good idea to feel anxious of a massive snake in the wild, or to run away if you see a lion that's escaped from a zoo (which is unlikely to happen as zoos are very safe!) – that anxiety will help you make good decisions about what to do to stay safe.

You cannot help it if some things make you feel anxious, and you yourself almost definitely have some things that make you feel **really** anxious.

What are some of the things that make you feel anxious? You can write them down in the box below, if you like:

Thousands of years ago, when humans first evolved, anxiety was necessary for us to survive.

As with the massive snake today, if a caveman came out of his cave and saw a predator like a sabre-toothed tiger and stood there wondering what to do, he would probably get gobbled up!!

Instead, without thinking about it the caveman's anxiety meant that he would either run away back to the safety of his cave (this is what I would do!)...

...or, he may fight back if the tiger started to attack him.

These reactions are known as fight or flight (running away).

Sometimes, when people are really scared, they freeze on the spot. Some animals, such as rabbits, freeze like this. It can be helpful as a predator is less likely to attack you when you are not moving and catching their attention.

When we feel anxious, changes happen inside our bodies too. When you feel anxious you may feel your heart beating really fast, or butterflies in your tummy. These changes are happening to prepare your body to run away, fight or freeze.

What feelings do you have in your body when you feel anxious?

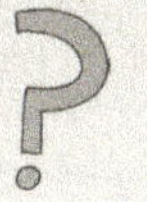

Luckily today, we don't have to worry about sabre-toothed tigers, but, for someone with PDA, being told, asked or expected to do something feels just as terrifying as it would have been for the caveman faced with a snarling beast. This is because demands make the person with PDA feel like they have lost their autonomy and the control that they need to feel safe and calm. They are preparing to fight, flight or freeze all the time.

Everyone's anxiety triggers are different. Some people get anxious about things that others find enjoyable – for example, lots of people are scared of heights, but some people like jumping out of planes or abseiling off buildings! Other people are scared of snakes, but some people like to keep them as pets.

What is really important to remember is that if something makes someone anxious, it makes **them** anxious, and we have to respect that.

Another good way to explain how anxiety affects people who have PDA is by using the Anxiety Bucket Analogy.

Imagine you are carrying around a bucket all day long, and every time something makes you feel a bit worried, anxious, annoyed, scared or uncomfortable a little bit of liquid goes into that bucket. Now, if you are neurotypical then you are lucky as your bucket has holes in it, so it can constantly drain the liquid away and your bucket rarely gets completely full.

For someone who is neurodivergent, their bucket does not have any holes in it, so every time they have a demand to deal with, or a sensory difficulty or social situation that they feel uncomfortable about, their bucket will fill up a little bit. Eventually their bucket will be completely full and there won't be any space for anything else. When their bucket is full this may be when the person with PDA goes into their fight, flight or freeze response.

When someone is really anxious, it means that they find it hard to think clearly.

DEMANDS

EMOTIONAL OVERLOAD

SMELLS

STRESS

NOISE

PROCESSING

SENSORY OVERLOAD

TOO MUCH TALKING

=

OVERWHELM

Most the children and young people I work with tell me that when their buckets are full they need lots of space and time to feel calm again.

When someone feels really anxious, they may not be able to say how they are feeling, and they may not be able to say what it is that they need to help them feel safe again.

When someone feels anxious it may look like something else. They may look angry, sad, shy or even happy because they are trying to cover up how they feel. Some people laugh when they are feeling anxious, which can be confusing. It does not mean that the person is laughing at you or thinks the situation is funny. Their laugh is a nervous reaction to a situation that has made them feel scared.

The best way to behave around someone who is feeling anxious is to try to remain calm because emotions can be pretty contagious sometimes! If the person feeling anxious sees that you are calm, this can help to reassure them. If the person sees that you are getting anxious or angry yourself, this may make them feel more anxious and angry.

ANXIOUS

ANXIOUS

ANXIOUS

No!

ANXIOUS

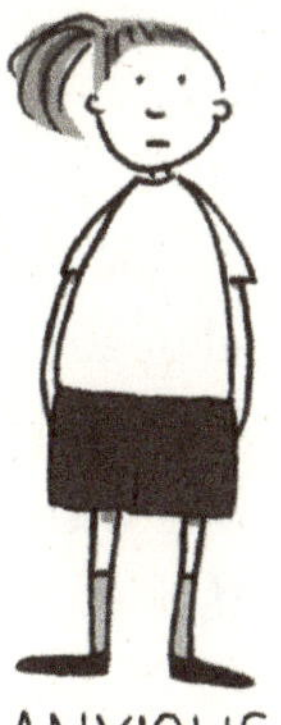

ANXIOUS

Chapter 4

Why Do They Get Treated Differently Sometimes?

If you have a brother, sister, family member or friend with PDA, you may sometimes feel that they get treated differently from you. It may seem like they always get their own way and that they 'get away with stuff', and this may feel really unfair sometimes. You may even feel that the person in your life with PDA sometimes spoils things like family days out or events, and this will understandably make you feel upset, angry or disappointed.

When someone with PDA feels very anxious or overwhelmed, they may do things like:

- shout
- swear
- hit

- break things
- ignore adults
- be unable to do things they are asked to do
- be bossy
- be controlling.

You may also feel that if you did those things, you would get into lots more trouble than they do!

If you are reading this because you have a sibling with PDA, then it is important to try and remember that your parents **will** treat you both differently sometimes, because you have different needs. It does not mean that they love one of you more than the other. It also doesn't mean that they always think that your brother or sister's behaviour is OK.

Let's have a think about other things that need to be treated differently.

PlayStations and Xboxes – both are very good game consoles, but PlayStations need PlayStation games and controllers to work, and Xboxes need Xbox games and controllers to work.

Android phones and iPhones. Again, there are lots of great Android phones out there but if you try and download apps for iPhones onto them, they won't work. Similarly, if you try and download Android apps onto iPhones they won't work either. There is nothing wrong with the phones, or the apps, but they need to be used on the right phones to work properly.

Dogs and cats. (Some people say you are either a dog person or a cat person, I personally love them equally!) If you try and take a cat out on a lead and get it to fetch a ball or stick, it probably won't go very well. Similarly, if you give a dog the freedom a cat with a cat door has, that probably won't end very well either! Dogs and cats also need different food to each other to ensure that they are staying healthy.

Petrol and diesel cars. If you put petrol in a diesel car, or vice versa, then the car will break down (unfortunately I speak from experience on this one!).

Plug sockets in the UK and plug sockets abroad are different too, so when you go abroad you need to take an adapter so that you can plug your things in to the wall there. It doesn't mean your devices are broken when you take them abroad, they just need the adapter to make them fit into the plug sockets in different countries.

DIFFERENT NOT BROKEN

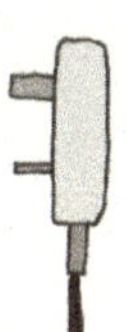

The point of the examples above, is that there is nothing wrong with Xboxes, PlayStations, iPhones, Android phones, dogs, cats, petrol cars, diesel cars and different plug types – they just all need different treatment to be able to work properly or thrive.

Phew!

Phew!

It is the same with people, we all have different needs, and we all need to be treated differently sometimes and have adaptations made to make sure we can be happy and thrive.

Remember, as I explained in Chapter 3, your brother or sister will just be feeling really overwhelmed by demands sometimes, and they won't be choosing to act this way.

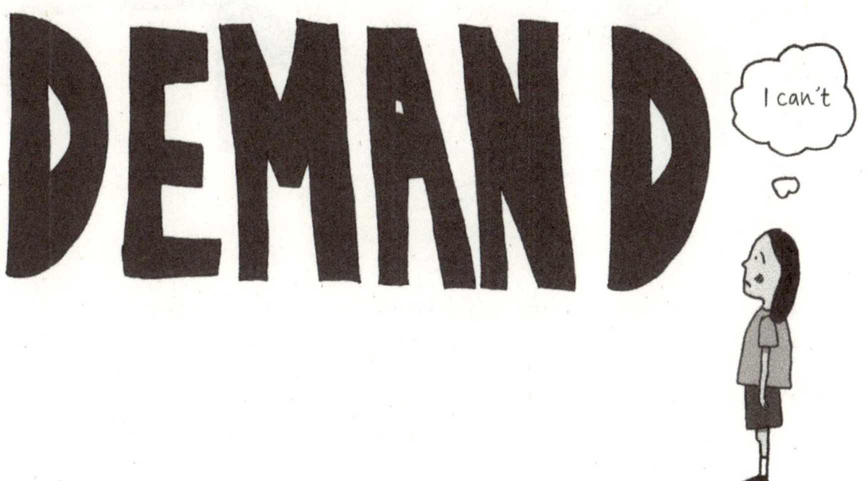

So, when your parents treat you differently to your brother or sister with PDA, it is not because they love them more or less than you, or that there is anything wrong with either of you. You just need your parents to treat your differently to make sure you are both supported and can thrive.

It is important to remember that your feelings are valid. It is OK to feel upset, angry or disappointed sometimes. What is really important is what we do with our feelings, so when we are angry it is OK to feel this as long as we don't hit or do things that can make the situation worse. Remember, you are only responsible for your actions and behaviour.

If you are feeling angry or upset, who could you talk to, or what could you do to help yourself feel better?

Finally, it is important to remember that there is no such thing as a 'normal' family. Every family has its ups and downs. Every family has arguments and disagreements, and at some point everyone who has a brother or sister has probably wished they were an only child!

Chapter 5

PDA-Friendly Language

Sometimes the way that we speak to someone with PDA may make them feel that we are being demanding.

Saying, 'Come outside and play football with me' or 'It's time to leave now' or even just saying, 'It's teatime' could make the person with PDA feel that they have little autonomy, and this will make them feel anxious. This means that they will then find it very difficult to do what you have asked or suggested.

We can change the way we speak to someone with PDA to make things feel less demanding. Here are some ways you can change your language.

Instead of saying 'Come outside and play football with me' you could say 'I would love to play football with you, do you want to be striker or goalie?' or 'Do you want to play outside? We could play football or cricket.'

Instead of saying, 'It's time to leave now', you could say 'We need to leave soon, can I help you get ready?' or 'I bet I can get ready quicker than you!' and make it into a game or a race.

CHOICES RATHER THAN DEMANDS

Instead of saying 'It's teatime', you could simply say 'Tea is ready if you want to come downstairs to eat.'

These are just suggestions, and you are not going to remember to do this all the time. It may not work every time to change your language either, especially if the person you care about with PDA is feeling really anxious. For example, if someone is feeling anxious and you ask them if they want vanilla or chocolate ice-cream it could be really hard for them to choose, even if they love ice-cream. Just making a decision can become really demanding when you feel anxious.

If someone is feeling very anxious even if you are following these recommendations, it may still be really difficult for them to do the thing you have suggested. This is when we need to give them lots of time and space to try and feel calmer again.

You could practise using this type of language with an adult, so you get used to using it. The more you do it the easier it will be.

Can you think of some examples of times when you could change your language to make it easier for you to be with the person you care about with PDA? What might you be able to say instead?

Chapter 6

PDA and Playtime

PDAers are great fun to be around, and they are very creative and funny so they can be brilliant to play with.

But we do need to remember that PDAers are autistic, and this means they will sometimes find it really hard to understand the 'right' way to behave around other people.

PDAers can also be really honest. Sometimes it may feel like they are being a bit **too** honest, and they may say things that sound rude. They are probably not meaning to be rude, they just say how they feel!

The other brilliant thing about PDAers is that they can have **amazing** imaginations! They love role-playing and are very good at it. They may prefer role-play games to games that have lots of rules to follow, like board games, which probably feel very demandy!

And then
we can swap

No

What games do you like playing with the person with PDA in your life?

Your brother, sister or friend with PDA may **love** playing amazingly creative role-play games with you, but they will probably want to make up their own rules!

It can sometimes feel that someone with PDA is being very bossy. This is because they like being in control. Remember this is because of their anxiety. They won't always understand that this is making you feel fed up or cross.

A good way to explain to the PDAer in your life that you are feeling a bit fed up or cross is to use one of the techniques below. These techniques help you keep your language simple and show that you understand how the other person feels too. So, you start by explaining the fact about the situation:

> **Fact**: When you don't let me choose my character I feel cross.

Then you show that you see the situation from their point of view:

> **Sympathy**: I know you like to have control in games.

Then you offer a solution to the situation:

> **Solution**: How about you choose first and then after 20 minutes I can choose a different character after that?

Or you could try this technique. First you explain what the other person is doing that you find hard:

> **When you**... shout at me

and explain how it makes you feel:

> **I feel**... like I don't want to play anymore.

Then you offer a solution to the situation:

> **How about**... we take a break and then try playing again later when we are both calm?

These are not magic solutions, but they may help you express how you are feeling in a way that is easier for a person with PDA to process and understand. The more you practise using these techniques the easier they will be to remember to use.

As in any relationship, you may have some things that you both enjoy doing with your brother, sister or friend, but it is perfectly OK for you to want to do different things sometimes.

It may be a good idea to use a Venn diagram to show what things you want to do with your brother, sister or friend, and to show that there are some things you each want to do on your own. In one bubble you put the things that you like or want to do, and in the other bubble you put things that your brother, sister or friend likes or wants to do. The magic bit where the bubbles overlap shows the things that you **both** like and could enjoy doing together. Here is one for me and my cat to show you what I mean!

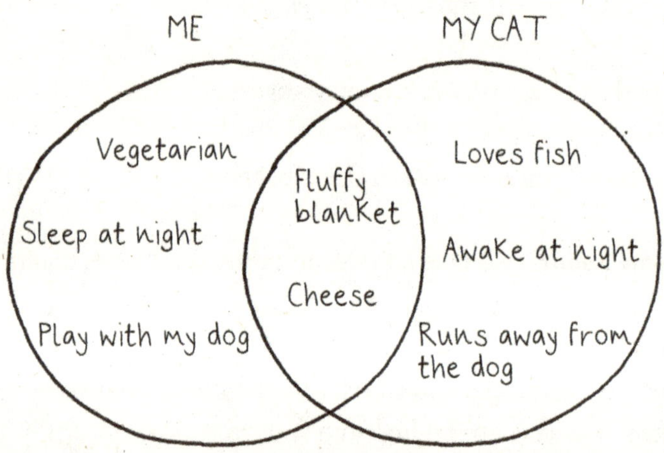

You could create a Venn diagram with the PDAer in your life, or do it on your own and show it to them to help you chose which games and activities you would like to do and when you would prefer to play on your own.

We have drawn a blank Venn diagram here for you to complete to show the things that you like to do, the things the PDAer in your life likes to do and the things you can do together.

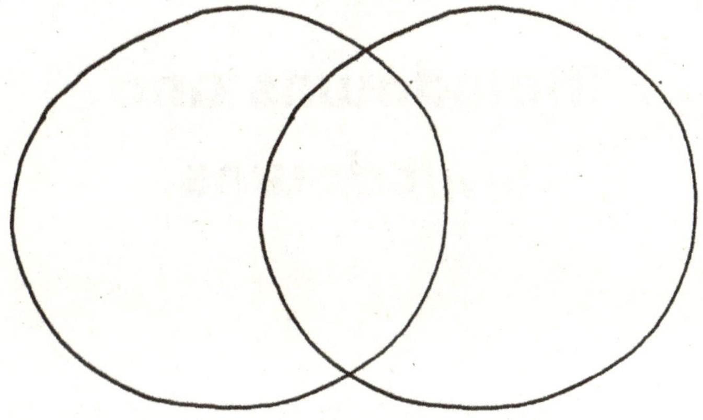

Chapter 7

Meltdowns and Shutdowns

Unfortunately, there will be times when a PDAer's anxiety bucket gets so full that it cannot hold any more anxiety. When this happens, the person with PDA cannot cope with anything else and they may have a 'meltdown' or a 'shutdown'.

When someone is having a meltdown, they may start shouting, screaming, hitting out, breaking things, etc. Although this can be very scary to be around, it is important to remember that this is happening because the person is feeling very, very scared too. They will feel like they have lost all control. The person may not realise what they are doing or saying, and they may not be able to remember what has happened afterwards either.

It can be hard for you to know what to do when someone you love feels like this, particularly when you feel scared and upset too, but the following may be a helpful way to think about it.

Imagine you go to a friend's house, and they explain that they have just rescued a new puppy. They tell you that the dog is very nervous and scared, and when you go to stroke the dog it growls at you and backs away.

Although you may feel upset and a little frightened that the puppy has growled at you, it is important to understand that the puppy is not being 'bad' or 'naughty'. The puppy growled because it is scared and anxious.

Hopefully, you would also understand that if you shouted at the puppy, or smacked it, it would get even more frightened. And if you did this again, the puppy would growl again and may even bite you. The situation would be likely to get much, much worse.

The best way to get the puppy to feel safe is to be very calm around it or to give it lots of time and space to feel safe and to trust you. Eventually, if you give the puppy lots of space and are very calm and gentle, the puppy may start to trust you and be able to come closer. The calmer and gentler you are with the puppy, the safer it will feel to be around you.

Although it can be really horrible to see someone having a meltdown, we need to understand that they are not choosing to act this way. Just like the puppy in the example above, the person is feeling very scared, and they need other people to help them to feel safe again.

Sometimes the person who is having a meltdown will need to have people around them, but sometimes they will need space.

When a person with PDA is having a meltdown, they may find it really hard to explain what is wrong. They may not know what they need the people around them to do or say to make them feel better, and they may say some things which sound unkind or mean.

It is not your job to make the person having a meltdown feel better, but it may be helpful to speak to your parents or a trusted adult so you can work out what to do to keep them, and yourself, safe.

Perhaps you can listen to some music or do something else to distract yourself?

Perhaps you can go outside and play in the garden?

Where would be a safe space in your house that you could go to if the person you care about with PDA was getting very anxious, so that you both had some time and space?

There are some things which will definitely **not** help if someone is having a meltdown. Things like:

- shouting back
- hitting back
- calling them names
- invading their space.

After someone has had a meltdown they can feel really awful. They may feel embarrassed or ashamed of the way that they acted. They may cry or even say things that can be hard for us to hear.

We need the person to understand that we still love them, and we understand that they acted the way that they did because they felt so scared and out of control. We should not blame them for their behaviour or say things that make them feel worse.

If your brother or sister shouts at you or hits you, sometimes you may do this back to them. You probably already know that this will not help the situation, and will probably make things worse. If this happens, then when you feel ready and the situation is calm, you could talk to your brother or sister and explain that their actions made you feel really angry, but you are really sorry and will try not to react that way again.

You could say, 'I am sorry I hit you/told you I hated you/called you a ***! but it made me so angry when you did X.

Next time you get angry or scared I will try to give you some space. If you can, can you do the same for me too?'

If your brother or sister is having a meltdown your parents may also feel upset and scared. They will be doing their best to keep things calm and safe for everybody, and this is when they may do things that you think are unfair. We have talked about how you can manage this in Chapter 4.

You may still feel really upset when things have calmed down and you may not feel ready to talk. You may feel angry or upset that you got shouted at or hurt, or maybe your things got broken. Remember, it is OK to feel this way, because your feelings are very important too. Talk to someone you can trust, either Mum or Dad or maybe someone at your school, about your feelings, particularly if you feel scared sometimes.

Not everyone who feels really anxious and scared has a meltdown. Sometimes, when people's buckets are full and they feel really overwhelmed, they have a 'shutdown' instead.

When someone is having a shutdown, they may go very quiet. They may not be able to speak or even move.

People have shutdowns when they feel overwhelmed and the environment is too much for them. It may not happen straightaway, but after the person has been somewhere that is too much for them, like school, a party or another really busy place.

A shutdown is also a kind of 'freeze' response, a bit like an animal that becomes paralysed when very scared.

Do you remember the rabbit we mentioned earlier? It froze when it saw a predator. This is where the expression 'like a rabbit in the headlights' comes from. It describes when a rabbit is in a road in the dark and a car is driving towards them. The rabbit just freezes in the middle of the road rather than running away because it is so scared of the car (which, like a predator, could hurt or kill it) that it cannot move.

Someone having a shutdown is like that rabbit in the road. Having a shutdown can feel just as horrible and scary as a meltdown even though it looks very different.

Another way to imagine a shutdown is that the brain is a bit like a computer that has too many applications open. The computer cannot cope with all the applications that are running, so it freezes and stops working.

When this happens with a computer we have to reset it. We have to turn the computer off, let it have a bit of time and then turn it back on but with far fewer applications open.

This is also what we have to do when a person has a shutdown.

We need to give them space and time, and sometimes let them have a rest so they too can 'reset' themselves.

How does the PDAer in your life act when their bucket is full?

However someone acts when their bucket has filled up, it is important to remember that eventually things will be calm again. Everyone will need to take some time to recover so that things can go back to 'normal' again, whatever normal is for your family and friends!

Chapter 8

Positives about PDA!

Thank you for reading this book. We hope you have enjoyed reading this book and learning a bit more about PDA. Here are some final questions, so you can reflect on some of the big things we've talked about!

What can be hard about having someone with PDA in your life?

What makes you feel better when things go wrong?

What makes the PDAer in your life feel better when things go wrong?

What are the things that you already do to help the PDAer in your life?

Is there anything else that you think you can do differently to help the PDAer in your life?

And, as you are lucky enough to have a PDAer in your life, you will already know that there are so many brilliant things about people with PDA.

What are your favourite things about the PDAer in your life? You can list them in the box below.

MY FAVOURITE THINGS ABOUT
THE PDAER IN MY LIFE

There are lots of qualities about PDA that we love! PDAers are funny, creative, adventurous, determined, honest and loyal. I love how well PDAers can pick up on what is going on around them – they are like truth-seeking missiles!

I like to think of PDAers as being: Perceptive, Determined and Autonomous!

PERCEPTIVE

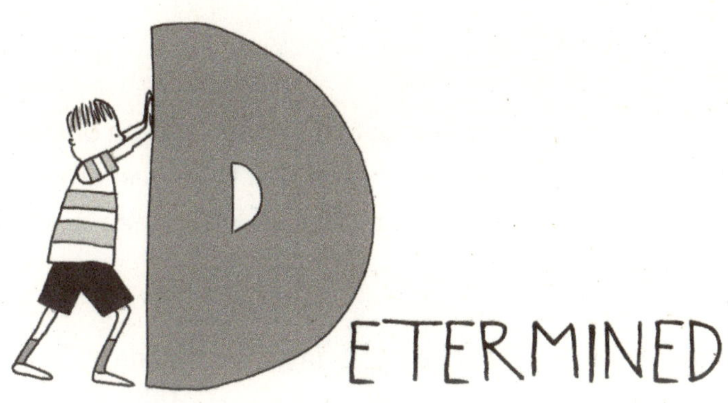
DETERMINED

AUTONOMOUS

If you could rename PDA what would you call it instead?

P:

D:

A:

We hope that you now have a better understanding of the person with PDA in your life, what makes them feel anxious and how you can help them and yourself when their anxiety feels too high.

Remember that there will be good days and bad days, but I already think that the fact that you have read this book makes you a pretty amazing brother, sister, cousin or friend, and the PDAer in your life is lucky to have you!